W9-CLQ-621

Acknowledgments

Crisp Publications and the National Retail Federation thank the following loss prevention and safety leaders for their participation in developing this book. The advice and feedback from these industry experts was invaluable in making this an effective and applicable resource for sales associates working in all types of retail environments.

William M. Bragg, Director of Security Training & Communications, Macy's East

O.D. Easterday, Safety Consultant, Alexandria, VA

John McNamara, Director of Loss Prevention, JCPenney

Bruce Van Kleeck, National Retail Federation

A Word from the National Retail Federation

The National Retail Federation is pleased to present the *Retailing Smarts* series. These books represent a whole new approach to developing training and educational materials based on national skill standards. Topics and information covered in these books reflect what retail employers across the country agree is needed to succeed and grow in a retail career.

We are proud of helping the retail industry pioneer the development of skill standards and raise expectations for a committed and competitive workforce. The *Retailing Smarts* series sets a new standard for industry-driven education and training that leads to productive and measurable results.

We encourage you to use this series and to let us know how these books are helpful to you, as a large or small company, or as an individual student or worker. With your feedback, the National Retail Federation can continue to create and improve the educational and training products that our industry needs to advance.

Tracy Mullin

Tracy Mullin
President
National Retail Federation

A Word from the NRF Foundation

The NRF Foundation, the nonprofit research and education arm of the National Retail Federation, is committed to creating the next generation of retail workers with competitive skills and career options.

The *Retailing Smarts* series will help retail workers develop the skills they need to perform well on the job and to take advantage of the range of options retailing can provide. We believe this series will help promote the image and opportunities—and recognize the professionalism and talents—of those who make retailing a career.

Training Directors: Crisp Publications can design training specifically for your work environment and employees. We can customize any of the *Retailing Smarts* lessons to reflect your retail format and work procedures. Crisp also publishes training materials on hundreds of other topics in easy-to-use programs using workbooks, videos, CD-ROMs and the web.

For more information or to order additional titles in the *Retailing Smarts* series, please contact:

Crisp Publications
1200 Hamilton Court
Menlo Park, California 94025
1-800-442-7477
CrispLearning.com

Contents

The *Retailing Smarts* Series

Retailing Smarts

Welcome to *Retailing Smarts*, a collection of educational materials developed specifically for the retail sales associate by Crisp Publications and the National Retail Federation (NRF), the world's largest retail association. The *Retailing Smarts* series is designed to provide training for the national retail skill standards, which were developed under the leadership of the NRF. Thanks to a collaboration of representatives from all types and sizes of retailers, the concepts, examples, and skill practice activities in the *Retailing Smarts* series are applicable across the retail industry.

Retailing Smarts provides a fun and easy way to learn and practice retailing skills in a self-study format. The materials can also be adapted by educators and training professionals for use in the classroom or corporate training programs.

Protecting Company Assets is one of the six NRF skill standard categories. There are two workbooks in the *Protecting Company Assets* set.

Protecting Company Assets

- ❑ Workbook 9: Preventing Loss
- ☑ Workbook 10: Promoting Safety

You may choose to complete only the lessons that are directly applicable to your retail situation or you may complete all of the lessons to ensure a well-rounded education in the national retail skill standards.

A Road Map to Success: Retail Skill Standards

What trainers need to teach, what workers need to learn, what employers can expect

What are skill standards?

Skill standards provide workers with a clear definition of what they need to know and do to be successful on the job. The retail skill standards describe the tasks involved for sales associates in the retail profession. They also describe how professional sales associates should behave in carrying out those tasks. This means workers now have a road map for understanding what is expected of them, how their performance is being measured, and what they need to learn to become proficient at their jobs.

Skill standards also provide a basis for selecting and training a skilled workforce. Employers use these standards to evaluate a candidate's level of experience and accomplishment in the skills that apply to their business. Employers and educators use skill standards to train people in a specific industry. This education may begin in a classroom setting, either prior to employment (as in high school, trade schools, or college) or in classes conducted by employers for workers they have already hired. Training in skill standards can also be accomplished by individuals who are willing to study on their own, using resources like this book.

Whether in a classroom or through self-study, learning about retail skill standards is only the beginning of the journey. Along the way, experiences with customers and co-workers will increase the understanding and mastery of these skills. Since each day brings new experiences, what began as training becomes lifelong learning. And when a person continues to learn, there is no limit to the successes he or she can achieve.

A Road Map to Success: Retail Skill Standards (cont.)

How were the retail skill standards developed?

Since 1992, hundreds of retailers, educators, and government representatives have participated in the development of skill standards for the retail industry, led by the National Retail Federation. This is part of a larger effort to define skill standards for all industry segments in conjunction with the National Skills Standards Board.

The initial retail skill standards have been developed for the professional sales associate for several reasons:

- The majority of North American workers enter the workforce through a job in the retail industry.
- The skills required for success in these entry-level positions are the same skills that will help workers succeed throughout their lives, both personally and professionally, whether in the retail industry or some other field of work or profession.
- In our current service-oriented and global economy, retailers need to attract and retain a dedicated, competitive retail workforce.

Which skill standards are addressed in this series?

The following retail skill categories are addressed in *Protecting Company Assets:*

- Identify and Prevent Loss
- Follow Safety Precautions

Detailed lists of the key tasks associated with *Promoting Safety* are included on the Learning Checklist on pages 8–9, under "skills demonstrated in the workplace."

How to Use this Workbook

Promoting Safety is divided into several lessons. The lessons are designed to take less than 30 minutes each to complete. A skill practice is included in most lessons.

Studies show that adults retain new skills more effectively if they apply them immediately to their own experiences. After you have completed the reading and any applicable skill practices for each lesson, put the materials aside and consider how you will apply this information to your work as a professional retail sales associate. If possible, practice this skill on the job before you start another lesson.

If you are using these materials...

On your own:

Find a mentor—an experienced retail sales associate—who will serve as your guide or counselor. After you complete a lesson, review your skill practice responses with this mentor to get additional advice and discuss any questions you may have. Having a mentor is an excellent way to find success in a new career.

Use the Learning Checklist on pages 8–9 to record your progress. You may even want to have your mentor initial the dates that you complete the skill practices. This completed checklist can provide strong evidence of your commitment to learning when you apply for that first retail position. Potential employers will appreciate your dedication to self-improvement!

As part of a class:

The Learning Checklist can be used by you and your instructor to monitor your progress as you work through the lessons. The instructor may want to review your responses to the skill practices and initial that you have successfully completed each lesson.

How to Use this Workbook (cont.)

If you are using these materials... (cont.)

On the job:

The Learning Checklist can be used in two ways if you are using these materials as on-the-job training.

First, your supervisor or a co-worker can observe your actions and initial the date on which you successfully demonstrated specific skills or behaviors. Including a brief description of how you demonstrated the skill will provide a basis for performance evaluation discussions.

Second, the completed checklist and notes about demonstrated skills can provide evidence that you are experienced in the national retail skill standards, reinforcing your credentials as a professional sales associate.

Skill Standards for Protecting Company Assets

In Workbook 10, you will learn how to apply the following skill standards:

Skill Set: Identify and Prevent Loss

- ❑ alert customer to your presence
- ❑ attach and remove security devices
- ❑ account for items after customer use of dressing room
- ❑ report stock shrinkage
- ❑ report security violations
- ❑ monitor floor merchandise
- ❑ alert sale associates to suspicious customers

Skill Set: Follow Safety Precautions

- ☑ report safety problems in the department/store
- ☑ follow emergency procedures
- ☑ maintain accurate records

Learning Checklist for Workbook 10

As you complete the workbook *Promoting Safety*, record your progress using the following checklists. These checklists can also be used as a basis for discussion with your instructor, supervisor, or mentor as you complete the skill practices and/ or you demonstrate the specific skills in the workplace.

Lessons Completed	Date Completed
Lesson 1: The Benefits of a "Safety First" Attitude	_____
Lesson 2: Stop Accidents Before They Happen	_____
Lesson 3: Common Sense—the Best Safety Tool	_____
Lesson 4: Help—There's Been an Accident!	_____
Lesson 5: Be Part of the Safety Solution	_____
Roundup	_____

Skills Demonstrated in the Workplace	**Date Demonstrated**

❑ Report safety problems in the department/store _____

Describe the situation and how you demonstrated this skill:
_____
_____
_____

❑ Follow emergency procedures _____

Describe the situation and how you demonstrated this skill:
_____
_____
_____

❑ Maintain accurate records _____

Describe the situation and how you demonstrated this skill:
_____
_____
_____

Protecting Human Assets

> **"Out of all the industrial accidents that occur, 85% are the result of unsafe acts, while 13% are due to unsafe conditions."**
>
> —Occupational Safety and Health Administration (OSHA)
> Compliance Handbook

When most people think of assets, their first thoughts are often of property, profit and loss, merchandise, and money. However, a store's most valuable assets are its employees and its customers.

Any customers in your store are in your store's care. Employees and customers are entitled to a safe and secure environment in which to work and shop. This workbook will explain how you, as a sales associate, play a crucial role in protecting the "human assets" at your store. Although many of the situations, problems, and solutions discussed in this book relate to clothing stores and departments, the same basic principles generally will apply to all types of businesses. All areas of the store must be kept free of hazards. As a sales associate, your best safety tools are good judgment and common sense.

The skills you learn in this book can also be applied to your home environment.

Promoting Safety

In the first lesson of Workbook 10, you will learn about the causes and costs of accidents in the workplace.

LESSON 1

The Benefits of a "Safety First" Attitude

> **Workplace safety has a direct result on corporate profitability. Employers are being squeezed by soaring medical expenses, lost productivity due to accidents and injury, workers' compensation claims costs, and damage to company property.**
>
> —David Arnold, vice president-research and general counsel, Reid Systems

Keeping an eye out for potential dangers in your store is not only good for your customers, it is good for you! When you develop a sense of your surroundings and learn to look for things that may pose a threat, you make your store safer for everyone—fellow employees included. Of course you cannot anticipate every accident, but there are many reasons why a sales associate should pay attention to issues of safety in the store.

Accidents cost money

The bottom line...Unlike money spent on inventory or wages, there is no return on money spent on accidents. Accidents always result in higher costs and less profit for the store. That can mean less income and benefits for you, the sales associate.

Hidden costs

What you don't see can hurt you...Sometimes a company's medical, worker's compensation, and insurance costs combined are less than the actual damage costs incurred by a single accident. Consider the cost of lawsuits, property damage, and interruption of services, and you will see that preventing an accident before it happens is in your store's best interest (and *yours* as that store's employee). You can't keep every accident from happening, but you can anticipate the ones most likely to happen.

Employee satisfaction

That "can do" attitude…When you take the initiative to improve your work surroundings, you set yourself apart as a person that can be depended on, a person that takes pride in doing the best job possible. You also gain the respect of your co-workers and of management. By being aware of your surroundings and doing more than just the bare minimum at your job, you will find that the work is more rewarding and can lead to additional opportunities and rewards.

The Benefits of a "Safety First" Attitude (cont.)

Customer satisfaction

A potential customer who hears of an injury due to store negligence is not likely to shop at that store. Everyone has shopped at a store that just seemed "like an accident waiting to happen"—a store where lazy or careless employees neglect to empty boxes or clear aisles, where shelves are dangerously overloaded, where lightbulbs are burnt out and others barely appear to be working. Any store that does not address the need for constant upkeep sends out the message that it doesn't care whether it wins a customer's business or not.

It only takes *one* bad experience to keep a customer away for good, and if a customer can see you're not interested in giving them a safe and pleasant shopping experience, you won't see them in your store again.

The attitude factor

Your attitude toward safety in the workplace can make a big difference in reducing hazards and accidents. Almost half of all accidents are the result of misplaced emotions and faulty attitudes.

Consider how the following can lead to safety hazards:

- impulsiveness
- irresponsibility
- anger
- failure to pay attention
- nervousness
- fear
- worry
- depression
- lack of rest

By keeping focused on providing professional service and the most pleasant shopping environment possible, you can avoid the dangers brought on by the following factors.

People usually get hurt because they:

- are not given specific instructions
- do not know what they do is wrong
- misunderstood instructions
- don't consider the instructions important
- deliberately disregard instructions
- haven't been properly trained

The Benefits of a "Safety First" Attitude (cont.)

Your best defense against workplace accidents and injuries is using common sense and maintaining a positive, "can do" attitude about providing a safe shopping environment. Additional guidance will be provided by your employer, who, at a minimum, must comply with provisions of the Occupational Safety and Health Act. This act was established to provided guidance and regulations for the safety of employees in the United States. In addition, many states and individual companies establish their own safety regulations and programs.

OSHA's role in safety and health

The Occupational Safety and Health Administration was created, in part, to:

- Develop mandatory job safety and health standards and enforce them
- Maintain a reporting and recordkeeping system to monitor job-related injuries and illnesses
- Encourage employers and employees to reduce workplace hazards and implement or improve safety and health programs
- Establish separate but dependent responsibilities and rights for employers and for employees to achieve better safety and health conditions

Many states have laws protecting employees from being demoted or fired for reporting safety violations.

*(Information on this page was reprinted from **A Manager's Guide to OSHA**, by Neville Tompkins, Crisp Publications, 1993)*

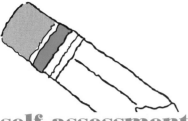

self-assessment: check your attitude

Directions: Circle true (**T**) or false (**F**) for each question.

1. You can anticipate every accident.   T   F

2. If a customer is injured in your store, the store is not responsible.   T   F

3. If you work in a clothing store, you don't have to worry about safety.   T   F

4. If a customer is injured, you should immediately move him to a quiet place.   T   F

5. Posting warning signs about potential hazards is all that you are expected to do.   T   F

6. In the long run, a store accident has no effect on your income and benefits.   T   F

7. Employees should have no say in the creation of safety rules—it should be up to the manager or owner only.   T   F

8. Turnover is higher when an employee is allowed to voice opinions.   T   F

9. Most customers are always on the lookout for safety hazards.   T   F

10. It always takes more than one bad experience to keep a customer away.   T   F

11. You should always admit responsibility anytime an accident occurs in your store.   T   F

12. If your store manager does not warn you of safety hazards you are not responsible for telling your customers.   T   F

13. You should not block off a spill unless you have called maintenance first.   T   F

Understanding the "Safety First" Attitude

The correct answers to the attitude check on the previous page are as follows:

1. F
2. F
3. F
4. F
5. F
6. F
7. F
8. F
9. F
10. F
11. F
12. F
13. F

Safety and liability are not always black and white issues. You may have to use common sense and sometimes go beyond what is spelled out in rules and regulations. When in doubt, it is a good idea to ask your manager or supervisor.

Stop Accidents Before They Happen

Your customers expect and deserve a place to shop where they don't have to worry about situations in which they might become injured. Some stores have custodians or maintenance personnel to clean up spills, broken glass, and other hazards that might result in injury to customers or employees. In other stores, the sales associates will be responsible for these tasks. In either case, you should use common sense and good judgment when such things occur.

It's a fact...Rolling clothes racks are a major safety hazard and cause many injuries every year. This is because the top bar is often higher than eye level, and a person who is paying attention to merchandise displays has no idea she is about to trip on the lower bar of the rack.

Pay attention...In addition to rolling racks, there are other potential hazards to consider. It's obvious that broken glass or spilled drinks are "an accident waiting to happen" and must be cleaned up promptly. Unprotected electric outlets pose a danger to toddlers who might wander away from their parents and investigate. Electrical cords dangling from small appliances provide a dangerous handle for pulling the item off a shelf. Cellophane-wrapped articles which are left on or have fallen on the floor, such as underwear, create an opportunity for people to slip and fall. Small, round objects, such as marbles, beads, or even batteries, create a similar hazard if spilled on the floor. These are a few of the things that you should watch for and take steps to prevent accidents.

Keep on the lookout...Many of these potential hazards can be eliminated with good old-fashioned common sense and a commitment to keeping things tidy. Make it a point to check the sales floor regularly and pick up any spilled merchandise, broken objects, loose electrical cords, and even litter.

When other safety hazards occur:

- Place barriers (such as yellow caution signs or orange safety cones) to keep customers away from the site until the problem can be corrected.

- Stay by the site (or asking another associate to do so) until it can be made safe.

- Call maintenance if appropriate, but take care to protect your customers by ensuring they don't enter the area and by letting them know the situation is being corrected.

- Make minor repairs or correct the situation if you are qualified to do so.

Stop Accidents Before They Happen (cont.)

The bottom line—keep an eye out for:

- Spilled beverages or food
- Sharp corners on display tables
- Broken glass or chipped glass fixtures
- Sharp objects that have been left around (such as box cutters or knives)
- Hot glue guns left out
- Loose adjustable shelving
- Improperly loaded shelves
- Overloaded shelves
- Merchandise that has fallen off the shelves
- Loose electrical cords
- Exposed electric outlets
- Empty rolling racks
- Damaged or poorly-constructed product packaging

Mrs. Stevenson loves to shop when the latest seasonal styles first arrive at the store. But one day, during the recent spring sale, she had to walk around several racks of blouses and dresses that had been just brought to the sales floor. Then, Mrs. Stevenson spied a table piled high with exactly the sweaters she was looking for. Excited, she took three steps and suddenly found herself tumbling headlong into the display. It turned out her foot had caught on the bottom bar of an empty rolling rack that had been unloaded earlier that morning.

The sales associate who had unloaded the rack rushed to Mrs. Stevenson's side to help. Although she wasn't seriously injured, she did bruise her head and had twisted her ankle during the fall. So although Mrs. Stevenson was fortunate not to have been seriously injured, she certainly didn't feel so lucky at that moment. After all, the accident could have been avoided if the rack had been removed from the floor right after it was unloaded.

skill practice: responding to safety hazards

Directions: Practice responding to safety hazards by checking (✔) the best answer for each of the following situations.

1. **What is the first thing you should do if someone spills soda or food onto the sales floor?**

   ❑ Call for a custodian

   ❑ Clean it up yourself

   ☑ Erect some kind of barrier around the spill or stand near the spill to direct traffic away from it until it can be cleaned up

2. **What is the first thing you should do if you find broken glass on the sales floor?**

   ❑ Call for a custodian

   ❑ Find a broom and clean it up yourself

   ❑ Erect some kind of barrier around the glass or stand near the glass to direct traffic away from it until it can be cleaned up

3. **What should you do if a shopper topples a pyramid of canned goods into the aisle?**

   ❑ Call for a custodian

   ❑ Pick up the cans yourself

   ❑ Check on the shopper, then erect a barrier around the cans until they can be cleaned up properly

4. What should you do if you find merchandise that has fallen on the floor from a display?

❑ Call for a custodian

❑ Pick up the items and arrange them neatly back on the display

❑ Secure the area with a barrier and report the situation to management

5. What should you do if you discover an electrical hazard?

❑ Nothing. Maintenance is probably aware of the problem

❑ Make temporary repairs as best you can

❑ Secure the area and report the situation to management for response by an electrician or qualified custodian

6. What should you do with empty rolling racks?

❑ Call for a custodian to remove them

❑ Remove them yourself to a separate room not used by customers

❑ Move them against a wall where they will be out of the way

Compare your responses to the suggestions in the back of the book.

Notes:

When you have completed the skill practice on pages 24–25, compare your answers to those in the back of the book.

Common Sense—the Best Safety Tool

Every job in a retail store involves the use of special tools and equipment appropriate to that job. As a sales associate, you need to know how to use those tools properly so that you can do your job safely.

For example:

- If merchandise is displayed up high out of reach, you should always use a stepladder (not a stepstool) or specially designed pole (such as a cherry-picker) to reach it. Never try to jump up to retrieve items.

- If you need to reach items stored on a high shelf, the same rule applies: Use a stepladder.

- For tasks requiring heavy lifting, many companies require the use of back braces or special belts to reduce the risk of injury to employees. This policy also helps a store control costs associated with worker's compensation due to injury.

- Some jobs may require the use of protective goggles, headgear, gloves, footwear, or clothing to prevent injury.

It is essential that you understand and observe whatever policies your company has in place regarding the use of protective tools and equipment. Taking shortcuts can result in a lifelong injury.

TIP

Lifting even light items can be tricky if they are oddly shaped or in a large box that is awkward to handle. Learn the right way to lift things—using your knees, rather than your back—and always holding items close to your body.

skill practice: working smarter—not harder

Directions: Review these two situations and circle the best response.

Case No. 1:

James, who works in a large store specializing in bed, kitchen, and bath merchandise, is having a very busy day helping customers during a big sale. A customer is stocking up on kitchen gadgets but is having trouble reaching a measuring spoon set hanging high on a display rack. James knows there's a stepladder somewhere in the department but is unable to locate it at the moment, so he finds a long-handled duster on a nearby rack and uses that to knock the spoon set off its hook.

What do you think about the way James handled this situation? (circle any that apply)

A. Using the duster was a resourceful way to attend to the customer's needs.

B James should have spent a few more minutes looking for the stepladder.

C. James should have asked the customer to finish her shopping and then come back after he'd had a chance to find the stepladder and retrieve the spoons.

skill practice: **working smarter—not harder** (cont.)

Case No. 2:

Sandra's job in an electronics store involves transferring large components from the back storeroom to the display counters and shelves. Sometimes, when she's working alone and can't leave the sales floor unattended, she gathers several boxes at once and carries them a few feet to the counter, where she will price them and put them on a shelf.

Is Sandra managing her responsibility wisely?

A. Yes—by picking up batches as large as she can handle, Sandra is working efficiently and getting the job done in a shorter time.

B. No—Sandra could seriously injure herself by picking up heavy loads improperly.

C. Maybe—while Sandra is the best judge of her ability to handle heavy loads, it would probably be smarter for her to transfer smaller armloads even though it will take a bit longer and involve more trips to the storeroom.

Compare your responses to the suggestions in the back of the book.

When you have completed the skill practice on pages 29–30, compare your answers to those in the back of the book.

When accidents occur, it is the sales associate who is often closest to the situation and it is important that you know how to respond. In Lesson 4, you'll learn what you should do in the event a customer or a fellow employee is injured.

LESSON 4

Help—There's Been an Accident!

Nobody really knows how he or she will react when a mishap occurs, especially if it is life-threatening. That is why you should think ahead about how you might respond if such a situation occurs. There are three traits a sales associate should develop now in case an accident occurs later.

- **Be Aware**
- **Be Professional**
- **Be Prepared**

Be aware

The first step is to become familiar with any store procedures that are in place. Because accidents happen suddenly and unexpectedly, you need to respond quickly. Do you (or does someone else in the store) know CPR (Cardiopulmonary Resuscitation)? Be sure you know whom to call if CPR is necessary.

It is also very important for you to know store policies or procedures for reporting accidents and situations that could cause them.

If you are the one injured, you should promptly report the work-related injury or sickness to your employer. If your store has a certain number of employees, you may have to file a workers' compensation claim. Some states have a time requirement on worker's compensation claims—they may have to be reported within two to 30 days following an injury.

If you are not sure if your store has workers' compensation insurance, or if there is a time requirement for claim filing, ask your supervisor or personnel manager.

Be professional

Whenever an injury occurs, keep the following points in mind:

- Don't panic. Remain calm, and reassure the victim that help is on the way.

- Keep an injured person lying down and quiet. NEVER MOVE THE VICTIM!

- Try to visually get an idea of the extent of the injury so that you can determine the appropriate next step. Avoid touching a victim since you may not know where the injury is.

- Notify store security or management as appropriate. As accurately as possible, report the injury, how it happened, and the present condition of the victim.

- Call 911 if the injury could be serious or life-threatening. If possible, inform management of the emergency situation before calling emergency services. When calling 911 (or security), tell the dispatcher which store entrance offers the best access to the injured person. Be very specific about your location and the injury. If the response team arrives at the wrong door, valuable minutes could be wasted.

- Always provide an accurate report of the incident. You may be asked to fill out a written form—be sure to respond to ALL of the questions. Failure to do so could result in the company being held liable if legal actions are later brought against the store. Turn in your report **immediately**.

NEVER move a victim who has fallen. Trained medics will take precautions before moving a person who may have suffered spinal injuries.

Be prepared

Many companies provide basic first-aid training for their employees. Be sure to take advantage of this training. Also:

- Ask your store to provide a small first-aid kit that can be kept handy, near the cash register. However, take care never to give anyone any type of drug—even aspirin.
- Take the time to learn CPR—you could save someone's life!
- Join a safety committee at your store if one is available.

**EMERGENCY
TELEPHONE NUMBERS**

Ambulance _____

Fire Department _____

Police Department _____

Taxi _____

Poison Control Center _____

Building Maintenance _____

Security _____

Building Management _____

Store Manager _____

If your store does not have an emergency phone list posted, use the form above or create one like it for quick reference.

skill practice: responding to injuries and emergencies

Directions: Review the following scenarios and note how you would respond in the absence of any specific store procedure for these situations.

Customer: "I have a terrible pain in my chest. I think I might be having a heart attack. Please help me!"

Your response:

If you know CPR and it appears the customer is indeed having a heart attack, ask a co-worker to summon security or management and then begin CPR. If you are not certified in CPR, but another sales associate is, have a co-worker locate that person.

1. **Customer:** "Excuse me—a lady in the next aisle just slipped on a spill of some kind, and I think she's hurt herself."

Your response:

_____

_____

_____

_____

2. **Customer:** "I just cut myself on a staple sticking out from a box of detergent. Do you have a bandage?"

Your response:

_____

_____

_____

_____

Compare your responses to the suggestions in the back of the book.

Notes:

When you have completed the skill practice on page 35, compare your answers to those in the back of the book.

No matter how much effort a company puts into keeping its stores safe for customers and employees, you and your co-workers have much to contribute to the process. In Lesson 5, you will explore what you can do to make your store an even better place to work and shop.

LESSON 5

Be Part of the Safety Solution

When it comes to safety, there is no substitute for a company-wide commitment, from the top levels of management all the way through the ranks. Every division—sales, management, maintenance, security, and administrative—has a unique view on how the store could be made safer for customers and employees alike.

Make it a team effort...Security professionals recommend that stores form a safety committee to share ideas on how to improve the shopping environment. A safety committee should include at least one person from each division. This will ensure a well-rounded approach to safety issues and solutions. If your store does not have a safety committee, speak with your manager or a member of the security staff about forming one. Chances are your initiative will be welcome and appreciated.

Customers are also experts on safety. When they point out hazards to you, take note and take action!

The following guidelines will help you plan, conduct, and evaluate a safety committee meeting:

- Choose a common problem that can be broken down into specifics and can be controlled by store employees.

- Limit discussion to a single hazard per safety meeting.

- Discuss reasons the problem exists and make suggestions on how to solve it.

- Develop a plan to eliminate the problem. Get agreement on the solution and actions.

- Decide how you will make sure a change has taken place.

- Prepare a summary of the meeting and distribute to all employees.

Safety Action Form				
Condition	Action to be Taken	Person Responsible	Target Completion Date	Date Completed

Develop a "Safety Action Form" so the issues can be resolved in a timely manner. Use the form as a checklist, and mark off the items as they are taken care of. This sample form may be copied and used by your safety committee.

Be a Part of the Safety Solution (cont.)

Find the time...some stores will allow the safety committee to meet during the workday as a paid activity. At other companies, employees may be volunteers who meet after hours on their own time to talk about safety issues. Whatever the policy is at your store, serving on a safety committee can be a rewarding and eye-opening experience. It also distinguishes you as a leader among your store's sales professionals, a person who cares about your customers and co-workers.

As the saying goes, "An ounce of prevention is worth a pound of cure." By getting involved in promoting safety where you work, you can truly make a difference.

TIP

One of the quickest ways to undermine a safety program is to neglect to report unsafe conditions. Whenever safety concerns are discovered, address them as soon as possible.

skill practice: being a part of the solution

Directions: Walk through your store or department and write answers to these questions. If you are not currently working at a store, complete the list while walking through one of your favorite stores.

Store Safety Walk-Through

1. Are there any boxes, racks, or other obstacles in the walkways, aisles, work areas, or exits? ❏ yes ❏ no

2. If yes, could these items pose a potential hazard for anyone, if left where they are? ❏ yes ❏ no

3. Who could be injured and how?

_____

_____

4. Are there any low-hanging shelves, suspended displays, or low doorways that customers or employees might bump their heads on? ❏ yes ❏ no

5. Do any of the racks, shelves, or other displays appear to be sagging or overloaded? ❏ yes ❏ no

6. Are warning signs posted to alert customers to specific risks? ❏ yes ❏ no

7. If yes, do you think their placement is effective? ❏ yes ❏ no

8. Are there any places you would add additional warning signs? ❏ yes ❏ no

9. If yes, where?

_____

_____

10. Are there any uncovered electrical outlets that could pose a danger to children? ❏ yes ❏ no

skill practice: being a part of the solution (cont.)

11. Are there any cords, carpets, tape, or other objects on the floor which might cause a fall or injury? ❑ yes ❑ no

12. If yes, what could be done to eliminate these hazards?

_____

_____

13. Are waste baskets available throughout the store? ❑ yes ❑ no

14. When you look around can you quickly spot an exit sign? ❑ yes ❑ no
Can you easily get to it? ❑ yes ❑ no

15. Is there adequate lighting throughout the store? ❑ yes ❑ no

16. If there are stairs, is their location clearly marked in case there is an emergency and they must be used? ❑ yes ❑ no

17. Are there fire extinguishers, standpipes, or hoses nearby that could be used in case of a fire? ❑ yes ❑ no

18. List any other potential safety hazards you notice:

_____

_____

_____

_____

_____

You are almost finished. Just complete the Roundup on the next page to discover how much you have learned.

In this workbook, you learned about the important role you play in maintaining a safe environment for your store, your customers, and your fellow workers. As a professional sales associate, you should always be on the lookout for ways to prevent accidents and be prepared to respond effectively if accidents occur.

ROUNDUP

Roundup: Promoting Safety

In this workbook you learned how important it is to use good judgment, common sense, and the proper tools, equipment, and procedures for the type of task you are performing. This will help your store create and maintain a secure environment for your customers, as well as for you and your co-workers. You also discovered ways you can help reduce the risk of injuries where you work. With that in mind, review the following items and check the ones that you feel you can now handle effectively.

- ❑ I am prepared to report safety problems to the appropriate person in a timely manner.
- ❑ I am prepared to correct a hazard personally, if appropriate.
- ❑ I am prepared to alert customers to safety hazards and provide assurance that the problem is temporary.
- ❑ I am prepared to keep customer service areas and exits clear and uncluttered.
- ❑ I am prepared to handle emergency situations and request help if needed.
- ❑ I am prepared to maintain a calm environment in an emergency.
- ❑ I am prepared to communicate information as it is made available in an emergency.
- ❑ I am prepared to complete appropriate documentation promptly and forward to appropriate individuals.

If you were unable to check one or more of the items listed above, review the pages related to those topics. Remember: the better you understand the issues and procedures with regard to protecting company assets, the more effective you will be in preventing and correcting potential problems. And that means a safe and pleasant environment for everyone.

Congratulations!

In Workbook 10 you have learned the important role that you play as a sales associate in making your store a safe place to work and shop. Being a leader in promoting safety will make you an even more valuable and successful employee.

Company Policy Checklist

Depending on whether your store is a small business, part of a large chain, or somewhere in between, it will have in place certain policies and procedures to guide you when various situations arise. Your manager or supervisor will no doubt provide an orientation to make you familiar with those procedures. Before you can truly master the lessons in this book on protecting company assets, you should be able to answer the following questions about your store:

What should I do if a spill or breakage occurs (notify management, try to clean it up myself, etc.)? Whom should I notify?

_____

_____

What procedures should I follow in the following circumstances:

- A customer appears to be having a life-threatening emergency, such as a heart attack.

_____

_____

- A customer gets a small cut from a staple while examining a box from the shelf.

_____

_____

- A customer trips and falls on the sales floor.

_____

_____

- Improperly stored merchandise falls onto a customer, injuring her.

_____

_____

What paperwork is required in the event I witness or am involved in an accident in the store?

_____

_____

Where do I get any forms that I am required to complete regarding accidents or injuries in the store?

_____

_____

How can I become CPR-certified?

_____

_____

Does my store have a written safety manual or a safety committee?

_____

_____

answer keys

answer key: responding to safety hazards (page 24-25)

Knowing how to respond to emergencies before they happen is a skill every sales associate should have.

1. **What is the first thing you should do if someone spills soda or food onto the sales floor?**

   ☐ Call for a custodian

   ☐ Clean it up yourself

   ☑ Erect some kind of barrier around the spill or stand near the spill to direct traffic away from it until it can be cleaned up

   Depending on the particular store you work in, any of these responses may be acceptable; however, remember that your first priority is to prevent anyone from getting hurt, and erecting a barrier is the best temporary solution.

2. **What is the first thing you should do if you find broken glass on the sales floor?**

   ☐ Call for a custodian

   ☐ Find a broom and clean it up yourself

   ☑ Erect some kind of barrier around the glass or stand near the glass to direct traffic away from it until it can be cleaned up

   This situation is similar to Question 1 above. Again, the most important thing you can do to prevent injuries until the glass can be picked up is to erect a temporary barrier around it.

3. **What should you do if a shopper topples a pyramid of canned goods into the aisle?**

   ☐ Call for a custodian

   ☑ Pick up the cans yourself

   ☑ Check on the shopper, then erect a barrier around the cans until they can be cleaned up properly

   Unlike Questions 1 and 2, this situation requires no special equipment or cleaning products. The best solution is to pick up the cans yourself.

answer key: responding to safety hazards (page 24-25) (cont.)

4. **What should you do if you find merchandise that has fallen on the floor from a display?**

❑ Call for a custodian

❑ Pick up the items and arrange them neatly back on the display

☑ Secure the area with a barrier and report the situation to management

Appliances found on the sales floor may be heavy, delicate, or otherwise difficult to handle properly. It is best to leave their removal to those who are used to working with them.

5. **What should you do if you discover an electrical hazard?**

❑ Nothing. Management is probably aware of the problem

❑ Make temporary repairs as best you can

☑ Secure the area and report the situation to management for response by an electrician or qualified custodian.

Once again, the best advice is to leave it to the experts!

6. **What should you do with empty rolling racks?**

❑ Call for a custodian to remove them

☑ Remove them yourself to a separate room not used by customers

❑ Move them against a wall where they will be out of the way

While any of these responses may be the most practical one in your store, your primary concern is to prevent injuries until the racks can be safely removed by a custodian or other designated individual. Even rolling the racks against a wall doesn't completely remove the risk that customers might trip over them; this is why moving the racks to a separate room for now is the best solution.

answer key: working smarter—not harder (pages 29-30)

Case No. 1:

What do you think about the way James handled this situation?

A. Using the duster was a resourceful way to attend to the customer's needs.

B. James should have spent a few more minutes looking for the stepladder.

C. James should have asked the customer to finish her shopping and then come back after he'd had a chance to find the stepladder and retrieve the spoons.

> The best answer is either B or C. As we discussed in this chapter, safety requires the use of the proper tools and equipment to accomplish each task. The duster was not designed to retrieve items from display hooks, and James could easily have fallen into the display rack or sent the spoons flying across the room, endangering others.

Case No. 2:

Is Sandra managing her responsibility wisely?

A. Yes—by picking up batches as large as she can handle, Sandra is working efficiently and getting the job done in a shorter time.

B. No—Sandra could seriously injure herself by picking up heavy loads improperly.

C. Maybe—while Sandra is the best judge of her ability to handle heavy loads, it would probably be smarter for her to transfer smaller armloads even though it will take a bit longer and involve more trips to the storeroom.

> The correct answer is B. Just as in Case No. 1 above, safety requires that employees use the appropriate tools and equipment to do their job properly. While it may seem more efficient to make fewer trips, Sandra could hurt herself by working harder, not smarter—even if she really thinks she's up to the task of carrying bigger armloads.

answer key: responding to injuries and emergencies
(page 35)

Customer: "Excuse me—a lady in the next aisle just slipped on a spill of some kind, and I think she's hurt herself."

Your response: First, erect a barrier around the spill to ensure that others will not be hurt. Then, remain calm as you attempt to determine from the woman the extent of her injury so you will be able to inform those who respond so they can take the appropriate action. Never admit the store's responsibility or guilt and never attempt to move the victim. Follow your company's procedures for dealing with minor injuries to customers. You should notify management and/or security about the incident to receive guidance on what further steps should be taken.

Customer: "I just cut myself on a staple sticking out from a box of detergent. Do you have a bandage?"

Your response: Offer the customer a bandage if you have one available. You should also locate the item/situation that caused the injury and take steps to prevent additional injuries.